G000149167

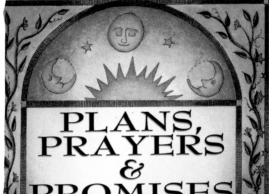

PLANS, PRAYERS & PROMISES

POEMS BY JILL LEMMING
ARTWORK BY LINDA SPIVEY

© 1999 Havoc Publishing
Artwork © 1999 Linda Spivey
Under license from Penny Lane Publishing, Inc.
Text © 1999 Jill Lemming

ISBN 0-7416-1102-3

Published by Havoc Publishing
San Diego, California

Made in China

www.havocpub.com

Havoc Publishing
9808 Waples Street
San Diego, California 92121

Wishing You the Best
of Everything.
With Love,

To achieve a measure of success,
you must first prioritize...
Make God your first intention,
and success will be
your prize.

We can reach the highest
mountain,
And swim the deepest sea...
As long as we have confidence,
In our strength and ability.

Have a dream and then pursue it,

Have a goal and then persevere...

Have faith in God to give it,

And see miracles appear.

It takes a "can do" attitude

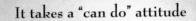

To make your dreams come true...

A special faith and wisdom,

For success to come to you.

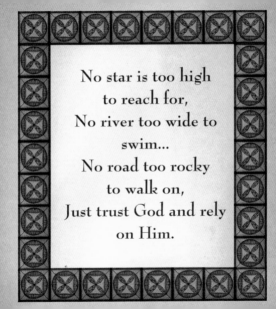

No star is too high
to reach for,
No river too wide to
swim...
No road too rocky
to walk on,
Just trust God and rely
on Him.

In our hearts are true desires,
That are buried deep inside...
We try hard to make a difference,
So the world will know we tried.

To aspire to lofty missions,
Is an admirable thing to do...
But give careful consideration
To what God has planned
for you.

God has goals for each of us,
And He works to intercede...
But we must find the wisdom
And faith in Him
to achieve.

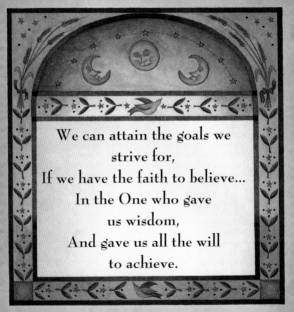

We can attain the goals we
strive for,
If we have the faith to believe...
In the One who gave
us wisdom,
And gave us all the will
to achieve.

Our dreams are
worth pursuing,
Our goals are
worth the cost...

But God is to
have the glory,
So our "selves" will
not be lost.

Encourage your ambitions,

And believe in them today...

Have confidence in knowing

God is with you all the way.

Follow God's
commandments,
And reach higher every day...
Be a light that shines
for others,
Let truth be your guide along
the way.

The things that we

aspire to

Are what lead us

to believe...

That we have the will inside us

To conquer and succeed.

As we aim for sweet
perfection,
And we realize all
our dreams...
Remember we are
nothing without trusting
The Creator of all things.

Life is worth
the living,
When we strive to
reach our goals...
And realize our
potential,
The very essence of
our souls.

Gracious Father
in the sky,
Creator of who I am...
Touch me with
Your power,
And let me be
the best I can.

When we reach a special milestone

That we strived for all along...

We know it's God's achievement,

And it's through Him that

we are strong.

God gives
us each a talent
To be used to
serve mankind...

Not to give ourselves
the glory,

But to keep His will
in mind.

As long as I am living,
I will strive to do my best...
I will give God all the glory,
On the road to my success.

Success is not by chance,
God gives us what we need...
It's He who reaps the harvest,
It's He who plants the seed!

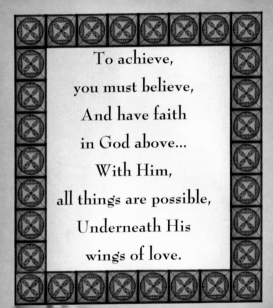

To achieve,
you must believe,
And have faith
in God above...
With Him,
all things are possible,
Underneath His
wings of love.

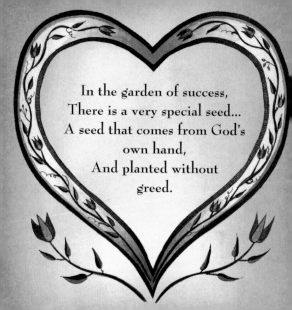

In the garden of success,
There is a very special seed...
A seed that comes from God's
own hand,
And planted without
greed.

To turn dreams into reality,
Reach farther than before...
Lift your dreams to Heaven,
To see the miracles
in store.

Many times we wonder

What goals we should possess...

Should we strive for earthly treasures,

Or just love and happiness?

The true measure of success,

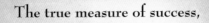

Is not the things we own...

It's the respect of one another,

From the people that we've known.

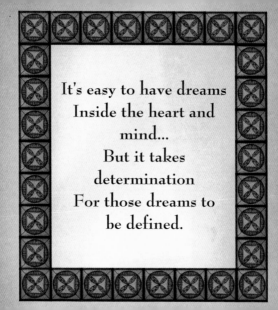

It's easy to have dreams
Inside the heart and
mind...
But it takes
determination
For those dreams to
be defined.

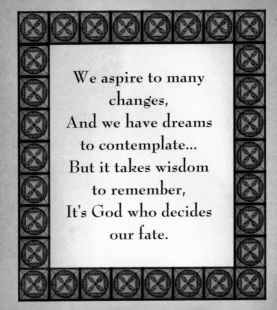

We aspire to many
changes,
And we have dreams
to contemplate...
But it takes wisdom
to remember,
It's God who decides
our fate.

I have many special people
Who have encouraged all my dreams...
People who have soared with me,
As the wind beneath my wings.

We should always have a vision
That will lead us to a goal...
Like a soldier on a mission,
Marching forward as we go.

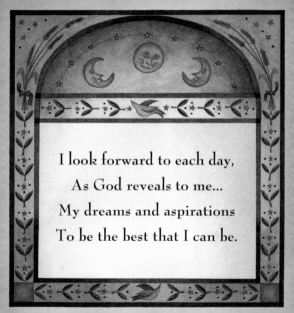

I look forward to each day,
As God reveals to me...
My dreams and aspirations
To be the best that I can be.

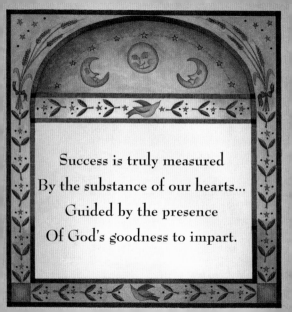

Success is truly measured
By the substance of our hearts...
Guided by the presence
Of God's goodness to impart.

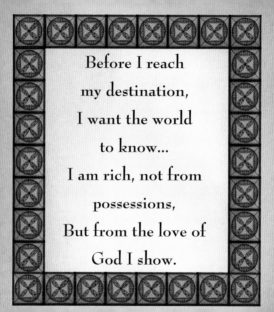

Before I reach
my destination,
I want the world
to know...
I am rich, not from
possessions,
But from the love of
God I show.

Follow your dreams,

Reach for the stars...

Believe in yourself,

And love who you are.

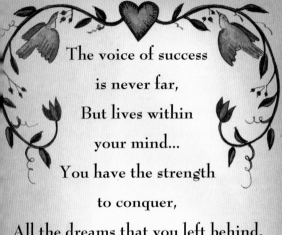

The voice of success
is never far,
But lives within
your mind...
You have the strength
to conquer,
All the dreams that you left behind.

Don't say that you
can't do it,
Don't say you'll
never try...
Believe in your
ability,
Or success will
pass you by.

Today I make a
promise
To try harder than
before...
To follow the
example
Of the people
I adore.

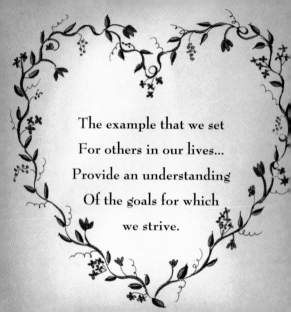

The example that we set

For others in our lives...

Provide an understanding

Of the goals for which

we strive.

We all have special people

Who help us reach our goals...

People who are mentors,

The instruments of

our souls.

Every day we look for ways
To be better than the day
before...
We have abilities to
recognize,
We have adventures to
explore.

Keep dreaming of tomorrow,
But be aware of the trials
you may find...
For the future holds
great promise,
If you leave your
mistakes behind.

Keep a journal of your dreams
To leave for your family...
To cherish through the ages,
For generations to see.

We should never give up trying

To reach our hopes and dreams...

For life is all about striving

And learning what happiness means.

Always give your best in life,

No matter what is lost...

For everything worth having,

Is worth the pain it costs.

If life were always easy,

We wouldn't have to try...

But life is worth the challenge,

And it's worth the tears we cry.

Goals are worth pursuing,
And dreams are all we need...
For in dreaming, we are striving
To be all God intended us to be.

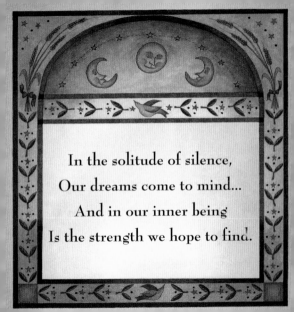

In the solitude of silence,
Our dreams come to mind...
And in our inner being
Is the strength we hope to find.

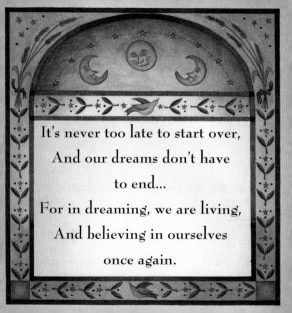

It's never too late to start over,
And our dreams don't have
to end...
For in dreaming, we are living,
And believing in ourselves
once again.

Follow God's own vision
To be what He wants you to be...
Find the root of your
intentions,
And the truth shall
make you free.

We should strive to keep a promise,
And to never tell a lie...
Because someone else will listen,
And find fault with you and I.

Be filled with aspirations,
And move closer to a goal...
And others will respect you
For being true to your own soul.

In the making of a

dream come true,

There has to be

a friend...

Who encourages you to persevere,

And loves you to the end.

Dreams and goals

are treasures,

To define our

very soul...

All we dare to measure

Is worth what the heart

can hold.

Reach for the moon
tomorrow,
And reach for the sky
today...
Reach for a dream to
follow,
Be true to yourself
along the way.

Aspiring and
achieving
Are more than just
a dream...
They're part of our
own being;
Success is a
wonderful thing.

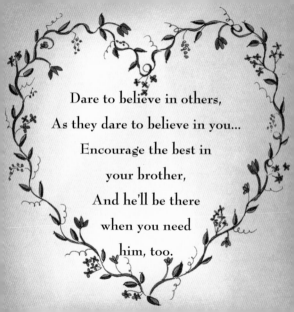

Dare to believe in others,
As they dare to believe in you...
Encourage the best in
your brother,
And he'll be there
when you need
him, too.

Never stop believing
In your dreams along the way...
We all need something special
To aspire to every
day.

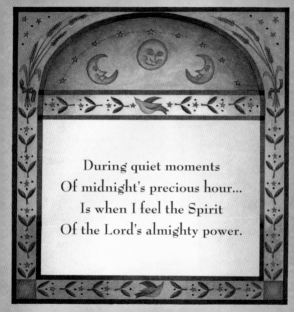

During quiet moments
Of midnight's precious hour...
Is when I feel the Spirit
Of the Lord's almighty power.

Now I sleep with true assurance
That the Spirit guides my way...
As the midnight hour
moves quickly
To the dawn of a bright new day.

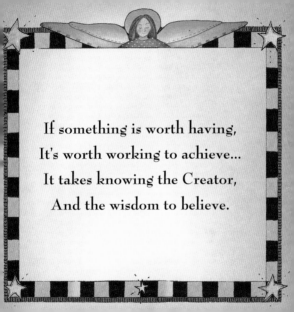

If something is worth having,
It's worth working to achieve...
It takes knowing the Creator,
And the wisdom to believe.

God gives us the ability
To weather every storm...
To find our dreams together,
And love to keep us warm.

Find the strength inside you,
And strive for a higher call...
Nothing is impossible,
With God you can have it all.

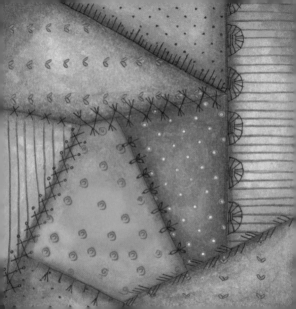